Bible Question Class Books

Bible Study Questions on Genesis
by David E. Pratte

A workbook suitable for Bible classes, family studies, or personal Bible study

Available in print at
www.lighttomypath.net/sales

*Bible Study Questions on Genesis:
A workbook suitable for Bible classes, family studies,
or personal Bible study*

© Copyright David E. Pratte, 2013, 2014
Minor revisions 2016
All rights reserved

ISBN-13: 978-1495397554
ISBN-10: 1495397556

**Printed books, booklets, and tracts available at
www.lighttomypath.net/sales
Free Bible study articles online at
www.gospelway.com
Free Bible courses online at
www.biblestudylessons.com
Free class books at
www.biblestudylessons.com/classbooks
Free commentaries on Bible books at
www.gospelway.com/commentary
Contact the author at
www.gospelway.com/comments**

Note carefully: No teaching in any of our materials is intended or should ever be construed to justify or to in any way incite or encourage personal vengeance or physical violence against any person.

"He who glories, let him glory in the Lord" – 1 Corinthians 1:31

Front page photo:

Mt. Ararat, where Noah's ark rested after the flood.
"Then the ark rested in the seventh month, the seventeenth day of the month, on the mountains of Ararat" - Genesis 8:4

Photo credit: MEDIACRAT distributed under Creative Commons license, via Wikimedia Commons

Other Books by the Author

Topical Bible Studies

Growing a Godly Marriage & Raising Godly Children
Why Believe in God, Jesus, and the Bible? (evidences)
The God of the Bible (study of the Father, Son, and Holy Spirit)
Grace, Faith, and Obedience: The Gospel or Calvinism?
Kingdom of Christ: Future Millennium or Present Spiritual Reign?
Do Not Sin Against the Child: Abortion, Unborn Life, & the Bible
True Words of God: Bible Inspiration and Preservation

Commentaries on Bible Books

Genesis	*Gospel of Mark*
Joshua and Ruth	*Gospel of John*
Judges	*Acts*
1 Samuel	*Ephesians*
Ezra, Nehemiah, and Esther	*Hebrews*
Job	
Proverbs	

Bible Question Class Books

Genesis	*Gospel of John*
Joshua and Ruth	*Acts*
Judges	*Romans*
1 Samuel	*1 Corinthians*
Ezra, Nehemiah, and Esther	*2 Corinthians and Galatians*
Job	*Ephesians and Philippians*
Proverbs	*Colossians, 1&2 Thessalonians*
Isaiah	*1 & 2 Timothy, Titus, Philemon*
Gospel of Matthew	*Hebrews*
Gospel of Mark	*General Epistles (James - Jude)*
Gospel of Luke	*Revelation*

Workbooks with Study Notes

Jesus Is Lord: Workbook on the Fundamentals of the Gospel of Christ
Following Jesus: Workbook on Discipleship
God's Eternal Purpose in Christ: Workbook on the Theme of the Bible

Visit our website at www.lighttomypath.net/sales to see a current list of books in print.

Bible Study Questions on Genesis

Introduction:

This workbook was designed for Bible class study, family study, or personal study. The class book is suitable for teens and up. The questions contain minimal human commentary, but instead urge students to study to understand Scripture.

Enough questions are included for teachers to assign as many questions as they want for each study session. Studies may proceed at whatever speed and depth will best accomplish the needs of the students.

Questions labeled "think" are intended to encourage students to apply what they have learned. When questions refer to a map, students should consult maps in a Bible dictionary or similar reference work or in the back of their Bibles. (Note: My abbreviation "***b/c/v***" means "book, chapter, and verse.")

For class instruction, I urge teachers to assign the questions as homework so students come to class prepared. Then let class time consist of **discussion** that focuses on the Scriptures themselves. Let the teacher use other Scriptures, questions, applications, and comments to promote productive discussion, not just reading the questions to see whether they were answered "correctly." Please, do ***not*** let the class period consist primarily of the following: "Joe, will you answer number 1?" "Sue, what about number 2?" Etc.

I also urge students to emphasize the ***Bible*** teaching. Please, do not become bogged down over "What did the author mean by question #5?" My meaning is relatively unimportant. The issue is what the Bible says. Concentrate on the meaning and applications of Scripture. If a question helps promote Bible understanding, stay with it. If it becomes unproductive, move on.

The questions are not intended just to help students understand the Scriptures. They are also designed to help students learn good principles of Bible study. Good Bible study requires defining the meaning of keywords, studying parallel passages, explaining the meaning of the text clearly, making applications, and defending the truth as well as exposing religious error. I have included questions to encourage students to practice all these study principles.

Finally, I encourage plain applications of the principles studied. God's word is written so souls may please God and have eternal life. Please study it with the respect and devotion it deserves!

For whatever good this material achieves, to God be the glory.

You can find Bible study commentary and notes to accompany these questions at
www.lighttomypath.net/sales

© David E. Pratte, August 25, 2016

Workbooks, commentaries, and topical studies for sale in print at
www.lighttomypath.net/sales

To join our mailing list to be informed of new books or special sales, contact the author at www.gospelway.com/comments

Assignments on Genesis 1

Please read Genesis 1 and answer the following questions:

1. Define "genesis."

2. Skim chap. 1-5 and make a list of things that begin as recorded in Genesis.

3. Who is the inspired author of Genesis?

4. **Special Assignment:** Research and describe the Graf-Wellhausen Documentary Hypothesis. List reasons to accept or reject it.

5. Why is a study of Genesis important to you? Is Genesis a book of children's Bible stories?

6. **Special Assignment:** Is Genesis intended to be taken as fundamentally history or legend/myth/symbol? List several reasons as evidence for your view.

7. Describe and explain each of the major terms in 1:1.

8. Find and list other *passages* outside Genesis that teach God created the earth, sea, etc.

9. Skim chap. 1 and list what God made on each day of creation,. Memorize this list.
1st day —

2nd day —

3rd day —

4th day —

5th day —

6th day —

10. What does 1:2 teach about creation?

---

11. **Special Assignment:** Research and define the "Gap Theory." When did 1:1 occur compared to 1:3-5? Note carefully Exodus 20:11; 31:17.

---

12. Describe the creation of light – 1:3-5.

13. Find 3 phrases that are repeated for each day (or most of the days) and explain the significance of each.

14. What happened on day two – 1:6-8? Define "firmament." Explain what it refers to.

15. What did God create on the third day – 1:9-13?

---

16. **Special Assignment:** What is meant by the phrase "according to its kind." List other passages elsewhere that refer to this concept. Explain the importance of this idea in Scripture.

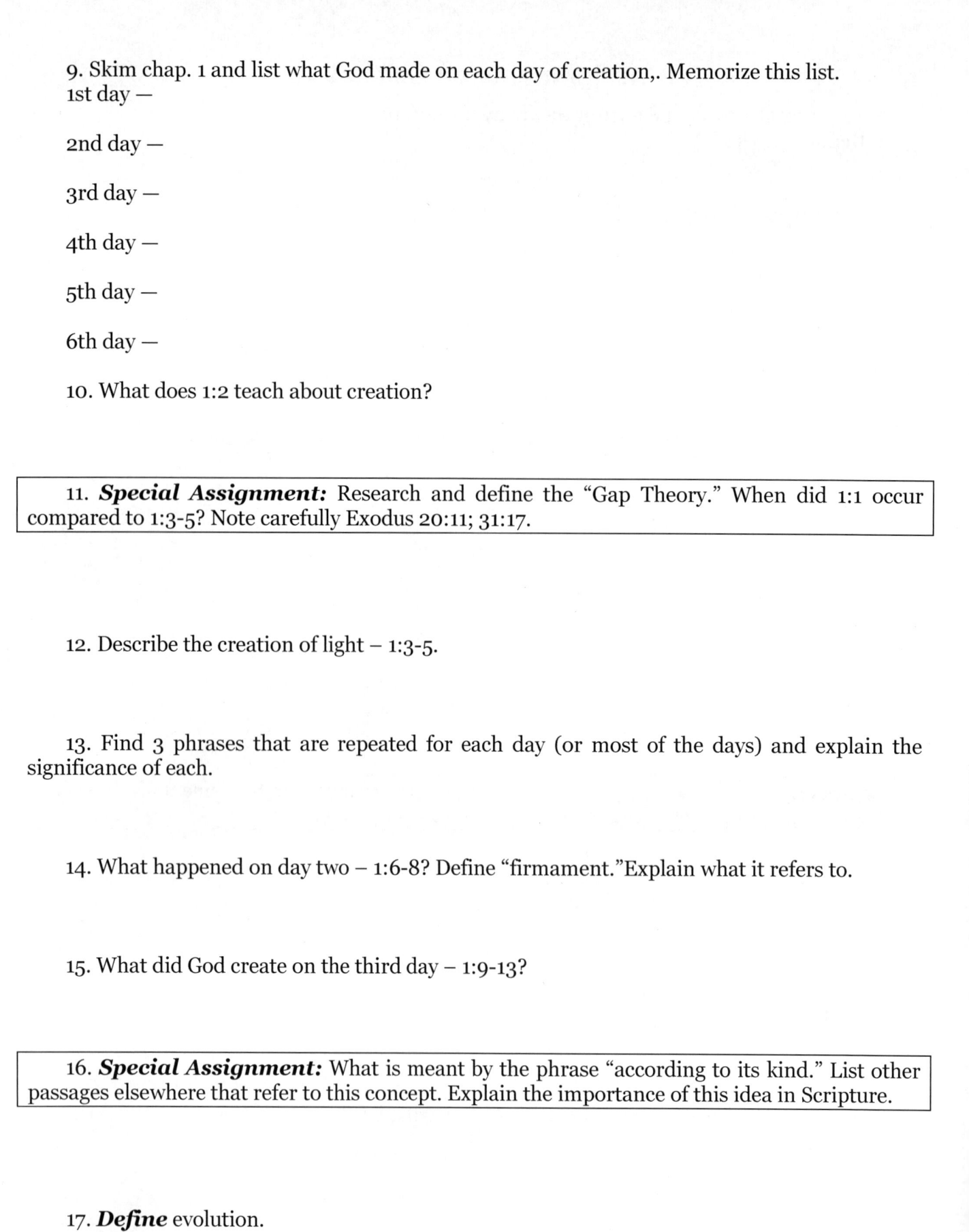

17. **Define** evolution.

Workbook on Genesis

> 18. *Special Assignment:* Explain how the fact things reproduce "after their kind" conflicts with evolution.

Note: Begin making a list of ways the Bible account of creation conflicts with evolution. Add to this list as our study of Genesis continues.

> 19. *Special Assignment:* Explain the concept of creation with maturity (i.e., did God create just seeds or mature plants, just babies or grown people, etc.?). How does this fit the creation account and how does it explain confusion about apparent ages in the universe?

20. What did God make on day 4?

21. Name 2 purposes to be served by the sun, moon, and stars.

22. What did God make on day 5?

23. What are we told about fish and bird reproduction that is similar to plants – 1:21?

24. What did God tell the fish and birds to do – 1:22?

25. What did God make according to 1:24,25?

26. What is again said about how they reproduce?

27. Find and explain expressions from 1:26 that show people are special in God's creation.

28. **Special Assignment:** Why does 1:26 refer to God as "us" plural, but 1:27 refers to God as "him" singular"? What does this tell about the nature of God?

29. List 2 other passages that show people are in God's image.

30. **Special Assignment:** Explain what it means to be in God's image. How is it true?

31. What special responsibilities were given to people in 1:28?

32. Explain what it means to subdue the earth and have dominion over animals. (Think: What kinds of activities would this authorize?)

33. What were people and animals told to eat?

34. How did God describe the things He had made – 1:31? What does this prove?

35. Make a complete list of all the ways you can think of that Gen. 1 conflicts with evolution.

36. **Case Study:** Some people claim that the days of creation were long ages or that long ages occurred between the days. List and explain Bible evidence regarding such views.

Workbook on Genesis

Assignments on Genesis 2

Please read Genesis 2 and answer the following questions:

1. Explain the importance of the fact that heaven and earth and all their host were "finished" and God's work "ended" – 2:1,2. How does this compare to evolution?

2. In what sense did God rest – 2:2,3? What lessons can we learn from the fact that God worked and God rested?

3. What Old Testament practice was eventually instituted that connects to the seventh day of creation (explain the practice and give book/chapter/verse for it)?

4. *Case Study:* Some folks believe that the fact God rested on the seventh day proves that people today must keep the Sabbath. Who rested on the seventh day according to Gen. 2? When were people first required to rest on that day? Does the fact the day is mentioned here prove we should keep the day today?

5. *Case Study:* Some people claim that Genesis 2 contradicts chap. 1. How would you respond (note Matt. 19:4-6)? Explain how chap. 2 relates to chap. 1.

6. How was the earth watered at first – 2:5,6?

7. From what was man formed – 2:7? How does this compare to what evolution says about the origin of man?

8. Where did man first live – 2:8?

9. Describe the trees of the garden – 2:9.

10. Name and describe the rivers in Eden. – 2:10-14.

11. What responsibility did man have in Eden from the beginning? What lessons does this teach us about work – 2:15?

12. What restriction did God place upon the man – 2:16,17? What consequences would follow from eating the forbidden fruit?

13. **Application:** What lessons can we learn from the fact that God gave man this command? What does this show about God and about man?

14. Explain why God decided to make woman — i.e., what need did she meet – 2:18? (Think: What is the meaning of the expression "help meet" – KJV?)

15. How did the animals get their names – 2:19,20?

16. For what purpose were animals inadequate? (Think: Why would the animals be inadequate for this purpose? What consequence does this have for the idea of evolution?)

Workbook on Genesis

17. Describe how God made woman – 2:21,22.

18. **Application:** What lessons can we learn from the creation of woman? What does this show about her purpose and nature?

19. List some New Testament **passages** that refer to Adam or Eve or the first man or woman.

20. In what ways would the creation of woman contradict evolution?

21. Explain what Adam meant about woman in 2:23.

22. **Application:** What lessons can we learn about marriage from Gen. 2:24?

23. List two New Testament **passages** where Gen. 2:24 is quoted and explain what lesson these passages teach in their contexts.

Page #11   *Workbook on Genesis*

Assignments on Genesis 3

Please read Genesis 3 and answer the following questions:

1. Summarize the contrasts/contradictions between evolution and the Bible teaching of creation as found in Genesis 1,2.

2. What animal was used to tempt Eve, and how is that animal described – 3:1?

3. What question did this animal ask Eve, and how did Eve respond – 3:2,3? (Think: Could Eve's sin be excused on the basis of ignorance?)

4. What did the serpent say would and would not happen if Eve ate the fruit – 3:4,5? (Think: Why would this appeal to a human?)

5. *Application:* What lessons can we learn here about Satan and about temptation?

6. In what 3 ways did the fruit appeal to Eve – 3:6?

7. List at least two other *passages* that show ways Satan tempts people.

8. What did Adam and Eve realize when they had eaten the fruit? So what did they do – 3:7?

Workbook on Genesis

9. What did the people do when God came to the garden and why – 3:8-10?

10. Find and explain at least one other Bible passage that shows the effects of guilt.

11. List two other **passages** outside Genesis that refer to this first sin.

12. What does the Bible teach about nakedness and inadequate clothing (use other Bible references in your answer)? (Think: What can we learn from the fact that the people were still "naked" when wearing the fig leaf coverings?)

13. What did Adam say when God asked him about his sin, and what did the woman say when God asked her – 3:11-13? (Think: What lessons can we learn from this about blame shifting?)

14. What punishment did God bring on the serpent – 3:14? Explain.

15. Since the serpent never ate the forbidden fruit, why did God punish him? What lesson does this teach us?

16. **Special Assignment:** What would happen between the serpent and the seed of the woman – 3:15? Explain how this came true and explain the significance.

Workbook on Genesis

17. Describe the punishments the woman received as a result of her sin – 3:16.

18. Find and list other *passages* that show wives should be subject to their husbands.

19. Describe the punishments the man would receive. What else was cursed besides the man, the woman, and the serpent — 3:17?

20. **Special Assignment:** How do the punishments for sin demonstrate God's intent for man and woman to fill different roles?

21. Find and list other *passages* showing that people die because Adam sinned. (Think: Were the consequences of sin suffered only by Adam and Eve or by their descendants too?)

22. **Case Study:** Calvinism says that, because Adam sinned, all babies inherit his guilt and are born totally depraved. What does the Bible say about this (consider Ezek. 18:20; 2 Cor. 5:10 and other passages in your answer)?

23. What name was given to the woman and why – 3:20?

24. How did God clothe the man and woman – 3:21? What does this teach about God's attitude toward adequate clothing – cf. vv 7,10? What does this tell us about the use of animals?

25. What change occurred in man's dwelling place and why – 3:22-24?

Workbook on Genesis

Assignments on Genesis 4

Please read Genesis 4 and answer the following questions:

1. What were the names of Adam and Eve's first 2 sons? What were their occupations – 4:1,2?

2. Describe the sacrifices each of these sons offered to God – 4:3,4. (Think: Did these events happen while Cain and Abel were boys or later? How do you know?)

3. List at least two other **passages** that refer to Cain and Abel outside Genesis.

4. What was God's attitude toward their sacrifices – 4:4,5?

5. *Application:* Did Cain and Abel know what kind of sacrifice God wanted? How do you know? What can we learn about worship from these events?

6. What was Cain's attitude when he knew God was displeased, and what did God say to him about it – 4:5-7?

7. What did Cain do to Abel as a result – 4:8?

8. *Application:* What lessons can we learn about persecution from this story?

9. How did Cain respond when God questioned him about Abel – 4:9? How does this differ from the proper attitudes Christians should have?

> 10. **Application:** What can we learn about sin from this study?

11. What punishment did Cain receive – 4:10-12?

12. What protection did God give Cain from being killed – 4:13-15?

13. Where did Cain live after God had stated his punishment – 4:16?

14. What was the name of Cain's son – 4:17? (Think: Many people wonder where Cain got his wife. What possible explanation is there? Cf. 5:4)

15. What did Cain build and what did he name it? (Think: What does this tell you about the number of people alive in Cain's lifetime?)

Workbook on Genesis

16. What practice did Lamech introduce – 4:19? Was this practice in harmony with God's plan (explain how you know)?

17. Name 3 of Lamech's sons and, for each one, tell what activity he introduced – 4:20-22.

18. What boast did Lamech make – 4:23,24?

19. **Special Assignment:** We have now observed 7 generations of people, counting Adam. Make a list of the practices or activities we have observed among the people which give evidence of intelligence, inventiveness, civilization, etc. (Think: How does this compare with the ideas of evolution? According to evolution, what should these people have been like?)

20. What did Eve name her third son and why – 4:25?

21. What did this son of Adam and Eve in turn name his son – 4:26?

22. What did people begin to do in these days? (Think: To what does this expression refer?)

Assignments on Genesis 5

Please read Genesis 5 and answer the following questions:

1. **Special Assignment:** Chap. 5 records the genealogy of Adam's descendants. Explain the value of such genealogies. Why did God have them recorded in Scripture?

2. By what name were the first man and woman called – 5:1,2? (Think: What significance is there is the fact that both the man and the woman were called by this name?)

3. What name was given to the next son of Adam who is mentioned, and in whose image was he begotten? (Think: What command of God was Adam fulfilling in 5:3,4)?

4. What can we learn from the fact Adam's son was born in Adam's image or likeness?

5. How long did Adam live – 5:5? (Think: How do you explain the long lives of people before the flood?)

6. What curse or punishment from God was fulfilled in 5:5?

7. Name all the men in the genealogy from Adam to Noah.

8. Why did Enoch not live on earth as long as other men? What happened to him – 5:23,24?

9. Find and explain another passage that tells what happened to Enoch.

10. What other Old Testament character did God treat in a similar way (give ***book/chapter/verse***)?

11. What man in Gen. 5 lived the longest, and how long did he live?

12. Why did Noah's father choose the name he gave Noah – 5:29?

13. What were the names of Noah's sons? How old was Noah before they were born – 5:32?

Workbook on Genesis

Assignments on Genesis 6

Please read Genesis 6 and answer the following questions:

1. **Special Assignment:** Make a list of passages outside Genesis that refer to Noah, and summarize what those passages teach. What can we learn?

2. What were some physical characteristics of some people in Noah's time – 6:4? (Think: What is meant by the sons of God marrying the daughters of men? Note Matthew 22:30.)

3. Describe what people were like spiritually (include several of the Bible descriptions).

4. What did God think about these conditions among people – 6:6? (Think: In what sense can God repent?)

5. What did God determine to do about conditions on earth – 6:7?

6. What classes of living things were going to receive the greatest damage – 6:7? (Think: Compare this to the list of animals created in Gen. 1. What kinds of living things are not listed among those that would be destroyed? Why are they not included?)

7. **Case Study:** Some people claim that God is too kind and loving to punish people for their sins. What lesson can be learned from Gen. 6 (include other passages in your response)?

8. How long did God yet wait until He took action – 6:3, and what does this tell us about God's character?

9. In contrast to other people, how is Noah described (note the phrases used) – 6:8,9?

10. **Application:** Name some lessons we can learn from the fact that Noah was righteous in a world filled with evil.

Workbook on Genesis

11. What had God decided to do to the earth and its inhabitants, and why had He decided this – 6:11-13?

12. What provision did God make to spare the good people? (Think: What does this teach us about the goodness of God as well as His justice?)

13. Define:
ark —

cubit —

14. Describe at least 5 characteristics of the ark Noah was to build.

15. Describe the size of the ark in terms of modern units of measure.

16. **Special Assignment:** Try to find measurements for modern ships and see how the ark compares.

17. What is a covenant, and with whom did God make one – 6:18? (Think: What is the covenant God made here — what were its terms or conditions?)

18. What people were to be saved in the ark (cf. 1 Peter 3:20)?

19. What other living creatures were to be taken into the ark and why – 6:19-21? What else was taken?

20. Describe Noah's response to God's instruction – 6:22.

21. **Special Assignment:** Name two qualities Noah had that were essential to his salvation, then show how we too must have these same qualities (cf. 6:22 to Heb. 11:7).

22. Explain 1 Peter 3:20,21.

Workbook on Genesis

Assignments on Genesis 7

Please read Genesis 7 and answer the following questions:

1. Why did God spare Noah – 7:1?

2. How many clean animals were to be taken on the ark, compared to the number of unclean animals – 7:2,3? (Think: Why would God say to take more clean animals than unclean animals? To answer this, consider the difference between clean and unclean animals.)

3. Why were animals to go onto the ark? (Think: How did Noah gather the animals? See 6:20.)

4. How long did God say it would rain – 7:4? (Think: What is meant by the fountains of the deep and the windows of heaven – 7:11?)

5. How old was Noah when the flood came – 7:6-16? (Think: Had Noah ever seen rain before? What effect would the sight of a storm have on him?)

6. What information is given that tells how high the water got – 7:17-20?

7. What happened to all the people and animals not on the ark – 7:21-23?

8. How long did the water prevail on the earth – 7:24?

9. **Special Assignment:** Summarize the evidence that indicates whether this was a global, worldwide flood or just a local flood.

Assignments on Genesis 8

Please read Genesis 8 and answer the following questions:

1. When and where did the ark come to rest – 8:1-4 (see a ***map)?***

2. When could the mountains first be seen – 8:5?

3. What kind of bird did Noah first send out and what happened to it – 8:6,7?

4. What kind of bird did he send next and what happened – 8:9? (Think: What information did this give Noah?)

5. How long did Noah wait before sending birds again the next two times, and what happened each time – 8:10-12?

6. When did Noah remove the covering of the ark and see dry ground – 8:13?

7. When did they leave the ark, and how long was this after the rain had begun – 8:15-19(see chapter 7)? (Think: What kind of changes would such deep, long-standing water cause on the surface of the earth?)

8. What did God say the animals were supposed to do?

9. What is the first thing we are told that Noah did after leaving the ark – 8:20? (Think: What does this tell you about Noah's character?)

10. What promise did God make to Noah at that time – 8:21,22? (Think: What application does this promise have to us?)

Workbook on Genesis

Assignments on Genesis 9

Please read Genesis 9 and answer the following questions:

1. What responsibility were Noah and his sons given – 9:1?

2. What kinds of food were men instructed to eat, and what were they not to eat – 9:2-4? (Think: What does this teach about the idea that it is morally wrong to eat meat?)

3. What are we forbidden to kill and what reason is given why this is different from killing animals – 9:5,6?

4. What punishment was decreed for the kind of killing that God forbade?

5. With whom did God make a covenant in 9:8-11, and what was the covenant?

6. What is the sign of the covenant – 9:12-17? (Think: Did God promise He would never destroy the earth at all? If not, what has He said about the future destruction of the earth?)

7. **Case Study:** Some people claim that God never changes, so He must do today what He has done in the past (miracles, forbidding work on the Sabbath, etc.). What can we learn about this from the covenant in Genesis 9?

8. Explain the meaning of 9:19. (Think: What does this verse teach that shows us whether or not the flood was world wide?)

9. What was Noah's occupation after the flood – 9:20,21? What did he do wrong as a result?

10. What did Ham do that displeased Noah? What did Shem and Japheth do instead – 9:22,23?

11. What happened to Ham's son as a result – 9:24-27? (Think: Who actually suffered the main consequences of the curse?)

12. How old was Noah when he died – 9:28,29?

Workbook on Genesis

Assignments on Genesis 10

Please read Genesis 10 and answer the following questions:

1. What does the account of Gen. 10 tell you about the historical nature of the book of Genesis? (Note: As you read various nations, use study helps such as Bible dictionaries, etc., to try to determine in what general areas these people lived.)

2. Name the sons of Japheth – 10:2.

3. Name the sons of Ham – 10:6.

4. What famous descendant of Ham is named in 10:8,9, and what was his occupation?

5. What kingdom(s) did he establish and what city(s) did he begin – 10:10,11?

6. What other nation, often mentioned in the Old Testament, descended from Ham – 10:14?

7. Name the nations that descended from Canaan – 10:16-18.

8. Where did the Canaanite peoples live – 10:19? (Think: What role did these Canaanite peoples and their land play in later Bible history? Study a concordance or cross-reference to help answer this question.)

9. Name the first four descendants of Shem through Arphachshad – 10:24,25:
(1) Arphachshad (2) _____ (3) _____ (4) _____ and _____

10. **Special Assignment:** Summarize in your own words what chapter 10 is about. Why is it important to our study?

Workbook on Genesis

Assignments on Genesis 11

Please read Genesis 11 and answer the following questions:

1. What did the people in Shinar intend to do and why – 11:1-4? (Exercise: Locate Shinar on a *map*.)

2. What did God say was His objection to their plan – 11:5,6? (Think: Explain what the people did that was wrong. Can you think of similar wrong attitudes of people today?)

3. What did God do to frustrate their plans – 11:7-9?

4. **Case Study:** Evolution claims that human languages began as a result of gradual evolution over millions of years. Explain how this story proves this is mistaken.

5. What name was given to the city – 11:9? (Think: According to our previous study, who founded this city?)

6. List the descendants of Noah from Shem to Abram. (Think: What trend do you observe in the ages of the men in this genealogy. What observations have we made that seem to be confirmed by this?)

7. Name Abram's two brothers, and name the son of one of them – 11:26,27.

8. What was the name of the region where Abram and his family originally lived, and to where did they move – 11:28-31? (Exercise: Locate these places on a *map*.)

9. Name Abram's wife and Nahor's wife, and tell what problem Abram's wife had – 11:29,30. (Think: What relationship was Abram to his wife — Gen. 20:12?)

10. Where did Haran die and where did Terah die – 11:28-32?

Page #25 — *Workbook on Genesis*

Assignments on Genesis 12

Please read Genesis 12 and answer the following questions:
1. What command did God give Abram – 12:1?

2. What New Testament **passages** refer to the call of Abram? What information do they add?

3. What promises did God make to Abram if he would obey – 12:2,3?

4. List at least two places in the Old Testament where these promises are repeated, and at least two New Testament **passages** that refer to these promises.

5. To what land did God lead Abram, and what did Abram take with him – 12:4-6? (Think: Canaanites were descendants of whom?)

6. What further promise did God give regarding the land of Canaan – 12:7? (Exercise: Locate on a **map** the area of Canaan and the places where Abram lived.)

7. Why did Abram leave Canaan and where did he go – 12:10? (Exercise: Locate this area on a **map**.)

8. What deceit did Abram ask Sarai to commit and why – 12:11-13? (Think: Was the statement Abram asked Sarai to make entirely false? See cross-references.)

9. What did Pharaoh do as a result of this deceit, and what consequences followed – 12:14-20?

10. List and discuss at least two Bible **passages** regarding lying and deceit.

Assignments on Genesis 13

Please read Genesis 13 and answer the following questions:

1. Where did the events in this chapter take place – 13:3? (Locate this on the **map**.)

2. What had Abram built at this place – 13:4? Describe what this is. (Think: Abram built these in many places. What does this tell us about his character?)

3. What problem arose between Lot and Abram? What caused the problem – 13:5-7?

4. What proposal did Abram make to solve the problem – 13:8,9?

5. List and explain at least three **passages** elsewhere that show the importance of peace and making peace. (Think: Under what circumstances may we give in to others to have peace, and under what circumstances would it be wrong to do so?)

6. What choice did Lot make and why – 13:10-12?

7. What were the people like in the area where Lot moved – 13:13?

8. **Special Assignment:** Using cross references, find and explain passages that show what results Lot's choice eventually brought on him and his family. (Think: What lessons can we learn about the danger of material attractions?)

9. What promise did God repeat to Abram – 13:14-17?

10. Where did Abram go to live – 13:18? (Locate on a **map**.)

Assignments on Genesis 14

Please read Genesis 14 and answer the following questions:

1. Who went to war and why – 14:1-7?

2. What was the outcome of the battle, and how did it affect Lot – 14:8-12?

3. Where did Abram live and who were his confederates – 14:13?

4. What did Abram do to save Lot – 14:14-17?

5. What two offices did Melchizedek hold – 14:18? Why is this significant?

6. What blessing did Melchizedek pronounce? What did Abram do for Melchizedek – 14:19,20?

7. Where else is Melchizedek mentioned in the Bible?

8. **Special Assignment:** Discuss the ways the New Testament says Jesus is like Melchizedek. What lessons should we learn?

9. According to the New Testament, what evidence is there that Melchizedek was greater than Abram?

10. How much of the spoils of war did Abram keep and why – 14:21-24?

11. Who did keep some of the spoils?

Workbook on Genesis

Assignments on Genesis 15

Please read Genesis 15 and answer the following questions:

1. How did God speak to Abram and what promise did He give him – 15:1?

2. What problem did Abram have regarding God's promise? What solution did he propose – 15:2,3?

3. What did God say about Abram's solution – 15:4?

4. What promise did God repeat to Abram in 15:5,7? Where else have we read this?

5. How did Abram respond to this promise – 15:6?

6. Name at least two places where Gen. 15:6 is referred to in the New Testament.

7. *Special Assignment:* What lessons does the New Testament teach based on Gen. 15:6? Some people claim this proves Abram was justified by faith alone without obedience. Had Abram obeyed God before this? What is the proper conclusion?

8. Despite his faith, what request did Abram make of God – 15:8?

9. What did God tell Abram to do to prepare for the revelation God intended to give – 15:9-11? (Think: Do some research to determine the significance of this act in vv 9-21.)

10. What did God predict would happen to Abram's descendants – 15:13,14? (Think: How was this fulfilled?)

11. What would happen to Abram's descendants in the fourth generation – 15:16? (Think: What is the significance of the expression "the iniquity of the Amorites is not complete"?)

12. What covenant did God make with Abram – 15:18-21?

Assignments on Genesis 16

Please read Genesis 16 and answer the following questions:

1. How did Sarai propose to solve the fact that she was childless – 16:1-3? (Think: What lesson can we learn from this about human efforts to modify God's plans?)

2. What problem arose after Hagar conceived – 16:4?

3. How did Sarai deal with the problem – 16:6?

> 4. **Special Assignment:** Muslims claim their religion came from Abraham through Ishmael. As we proceed, note what lessons we can learn about Ishmael's relation to the promises God made to Abraham.

5. Who found Hagar and where was she – 16:7?

6. What did the angel tell Hagar to do – 16:8,9?

7. What promise did he give her – 16:10? (Think: How was this prophecy fulfilled?)

8. What name was given to Hagar's child – 16:11?

9. What did the angel predict about the child's nature and future – 16:12? (Think: Again, does this refer primarily to Ishmael himself or to his descendants?)

10. What name was given to the place where this promise was given, and what does that name mean – 16:13,14? (Think: What lessons can we learn from the meaning of this name?)

11. How old was Abram when Hagar's son was born – 16:15,16?

Workbook on Genesis

Assignments on Genesis 17

Please read Genesis 17 and answer the following questions:

1. How old was Abram when the events in this chapter occurred (17:1), and how long was it after Ishmael had been born (16:16)?

2. What name is used for God (17:1), and what does this tell us about God's character?

3. What promises were made regarding Abram's descendants – 17:2-8? (Think: Explain the fulfillment of the promise of a multitude of nations coming from Abram.)

4. What change was made in Abram's name? (Think: What were the meanings of the old name and the new name? Why was the change made?)

5. What sign should Abraham's descendants observe – 17:9-13? When should it be done?

6. **Special Assignment:** Using cross-references or a concordance, list and explain *passages* that tell whether or not people must still be circumcised under the New Testament. (Think: In what sense was this an "everlasting" covenant?)

7. What change was made in Sarai's name – 17:15,16? What promise did God make regarding her? (Think: See if you can determine the significance in her name change.)

8. **Case Study:** Some people say, "There's nothing in a name." What can we learn from this chapter about the attitude of God toward names?

9. How did Abraham react to God's promise regarding Sarah, and what request did he make – 17:17,18?

10. What name did God say Abraham should give the promised son, and what promise did God make regarding him – 17:19-21?

11. How did Abraham demonstrate obedience to God's command – 17:23-27?

Assignments on Genesis 18

Please read Genesis 18 and answer the following questions:

1. Who visited Abraham – 18:1,2? (Think: Who did the visitors turn out to be?)

2. What acts of hospitality did Abraham offer to the visitors – 18:2-8? (Think: What can we learn about eating these various kinds of food?)

3. **Special Assignment:** What do other **passages** teach us regarding hospitality or kindness to strangers?

4. What prediction did the visitors make regarding Sarah – 18:9,10?

5. How did Sarah react to this prediction and why – 18:11,12?

6. What did God say about Sarah's reaction? How did Sarah then respond – 18:13-15?

7. What did God know Abraham would do for his household and children – 18:19?

8. **Special Assignment:** List and explain two other **passages** showing the duty of fathers toward their families.

9. What did God say He intended to do regarding Sodom and Gomorrah – 18:20,21?

10. What request did Abraham originally make regarding Sodom, and what was his final request which God granted – 18:23-33? (Think: What reason did Abraham offer for his request? Whom was he primarily concerned about?)

11. **Special Assignment:** List and explain two **passages** about the power of prayer.

Workbook on Genesis

Assignments on Genesis 19

Please read Genesis 19 and answer the following questions:

1. Who met the angels at Sodom and what did he do for them – 19:1-3?

2. Who came to the house later and what did they want to do – 19:4,5? (Think: What is the meaning of the expression "know them," as used in older translations? Study newer translations and see cross-references.)

3. **Application:** Find and explain 2 other **passages** that show God's attitude toward homosexual practices. (Note: Look up "sodomy" in a dictionary and see how the name of this city came to relate to the evil practice described here.)

4. How did Lot attempt to discourage the men of the city – 19:6-8? (Think: Observations?)

5. What did the angels do to protect Lot from the people – 19:9-11?

6. Why had these angels come to Sodom, and how did this event help accomplish their purpose — cf. 18:20,21?

7. What did the angels warn Lot to do and why – 19:12,13?

8. Whom did Lot try to warn to leave, and how did they react – 19:14? (Think: What does this show about other family members Lot had besides his wife and two daughters?)

9. What further instructions did the angels give Lot – 19:15-17?

10. What concession did they make to Lot – 19:18-22?

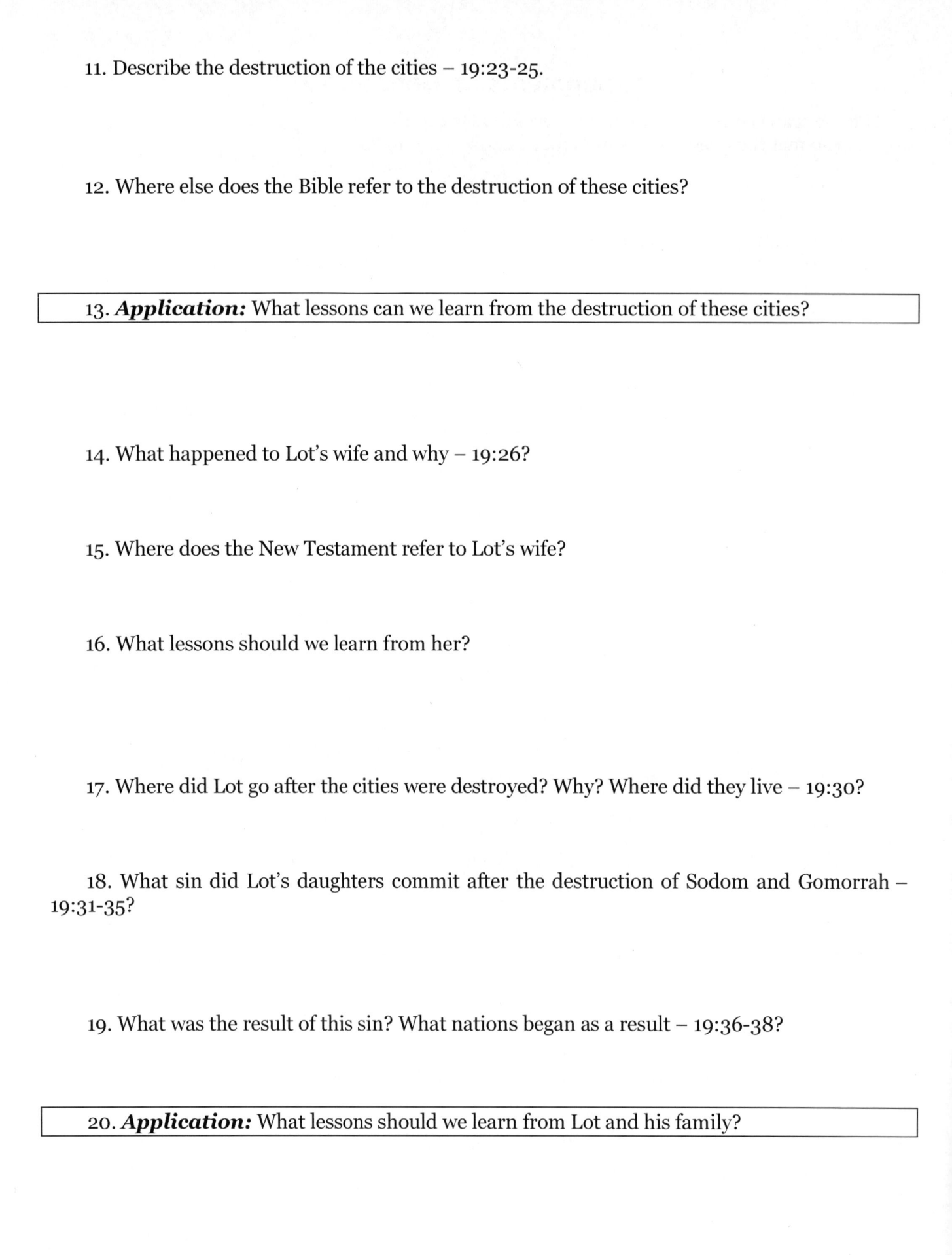

11. Describe the destruction of the cities – 19:23-25.

12. Where else does the Bible refer to the destruction of these cities?

13. *Application:* What lessons can we learn from the destruction of these cities?

14. What happened to Lot's wife and why – 19:26?

15. Where does the New Testament refer to Lot's wife?

16. What lessons should we learn from her?

17. Where did Lot go after the cities were destroyed? Why? Where did they live – 19:30?

18. What sin did Lot's daughters commit after the destruction of Sodom and Gomorrah – 19:31-35?

19. What was the result of this sin? What nations began as a result – 19:36-38?

20. *Application:* What lessons should we learn from Lot and his family?

Workbook on Genesis

Assignments on Genesis 20

Please read Gen. 20 and answer the following questions:

1. To where did Abraham move next – 20:1?

2. Who was king in that area – 20:2?

3. What deceit did Abraham do? Where else in Genesis did he do a similar thing?

4. What did God say to the king about it and how did the king respond – 20:3?

5. What did God say He had done to keep the king from sinning, and what did He tell the king to do about the situation – 20:4-7?

6. What did the king say to Abraham about it – 20:8-10?

7. How did Abraham justify his conduct – 20:11,12? (Think: As the situation unfolded, who appears to have the greater fear of God, Abraham or Abimelech?)

8. What arrangement did Sarah and Abraham have that led to this deceit – 20:13? (Think: How old was Sarah at this time and what does that tell you about her?)

9. What did Abimelech do to compensate Abraham and Sarah – 20:14-16?

10. What did Abraham do for Abimelech and his people? Why was this needed – 20:17,18?

Workbook on Genesis

Assignments on Genesis 21

Please read Gen. 21 and answer the following questions:

1. How old was Abraham when the promised son was born – 21:1-5? What name was given to the child? (Think: What did the son's name mean?)

2. Describe Sarah's reaction to the birth of her son – 21:6,7. (Think: What can we learn?)

3. **Special Assignment:** What promises and commands of God were fulfilled in – 21:1-7? Discuss possible reasons why God might have waited so long to give this child.

4. What problem arose regarding Ishmael – 21:8,9?

5. What did Sarah want to do with Ishmael and why – 21:10?

6. How did Abraham feel about Sarah's intention regarding Ishmael, and what did God say about it – 21:11,12? (Think: What lessons can we learn about Abraham, Sarah, and God?)

7. What did God promise to do for Ishmael – 21:13?

8. **Special Assignment:** Where is this event referred to in the New Testament, and what lessons is it used to teach?

9. When Hagar and Ishmael left, what problem did they face – 21:14-16? (Think: How old was Ishmael at this time?)

10. How was the problem solved? What promises did God repeat to Hagar – 21:17-19?

11. What happened to Ishmael as he grew – 21:20,21?

12. What problem had developed between Abraham and some servants of Abimelech – 21:22-26? (Think: Who was Abimelech?)

13. What agreement did Abraham and Abimelech make, how did they symbolize it, and what was the place named – 21:27-34?

Workbook on Genesis

Assignments on Genesis 22

Please read Genesis 22 and answer the following questions:

1. What test did God give Abraham – 22:1,2?

2. **Special Assignment:** Why would this be hard for Abraham to do (remember all we have studied regarding Isaac's birth and the promises God had made regarding him).

3. Despite the difficulties, how did Abraham show his willingness to obey – 22:3,4? (Think: What applications can we make to people who postpone or neglect to obey God?)

4. What question did Isaac ask regarding the proceedings and how did Abraham answer – 22:5-8? (Think: In what sense was Abraham's answer correct?)

5. How far did Abraham go with the sacrifice, and why did he stop – 22:9-12?

6. What did he offer instead of Isaac – 22:13?

7. What did God say regarding Abraham's willingness to offer Isaac – 22:14-18? (Think: What sacrifices does God expect us to make for Him?)

8. Find and list verses in Heb. 11 that refer to this event. According to these verses, what did Abraham believe God could do if he did kill Isaac?

9. **Application:** If Abraham is an example of faith, what can we learn from him about the relationship between faith and obedience?

10. List similarities between the sacrifice of Isaac and the death of Jesus.

11. Which of Abraham's relatives was also having numerous descendants – 22:20-24?

Workbook on Genesis

Assignments on Genesis 23

Please read Gen. 23 and answer the following questions:

1. How old was Sarah when she died, and where did she die – 23:1,2? (Think: How old was Isaac when His mother died?)

2. **Special Assignment:** Consider the Bible descriptions and passages about Sarah, and discuss the ways in which Sarah was one of the great women of the Bible.

3. From what group of people did Abraham want to obtain a burial place – 23:3?

4. When the people said they would give him a burial place, what place did he choose and to whom did it belong – 23:4-9?

5. What did the owner of the property offer to do for Abraham, and what arrangement was finally made for Abraham to obtain it – 23:10-20?

6. **Special Assignment:** Use cross-references and list the names of other people who were later buried in this same place.

Workbook on Genesis

Assignments on Genesis 24

Please read Genesis 24 and answer the following questions:

1. What did Abraham want to obtain for his son Isaac – 24:1-4?

2. Whom did he send to find her?

3. From what people did he want a wife for Isaac and from whom did he not want her to be?

4. **Application:** What can we learn from Abraham's concern about a proper wife for his son?

5. What did Abraham make his servant do to assure he would follow Abraham's wishes, and what did Abraham say God would do to help the servant – 24:5-9?

6. If the girl the servant found would not agree to marry Isaac, what was the servant to do and what was he not to do?

7. What provisions did the servant make for his journey, and to where did he travel – 24:10?

8. When he arrived, what did the servant do first to assure the success of his mission, and what lesson can we learn – 24:12?

9. Describe the method the servant decided to use to identify the correct woman as a wife for Isaac – 24:13,14. (Think: Why was this a good plan?)

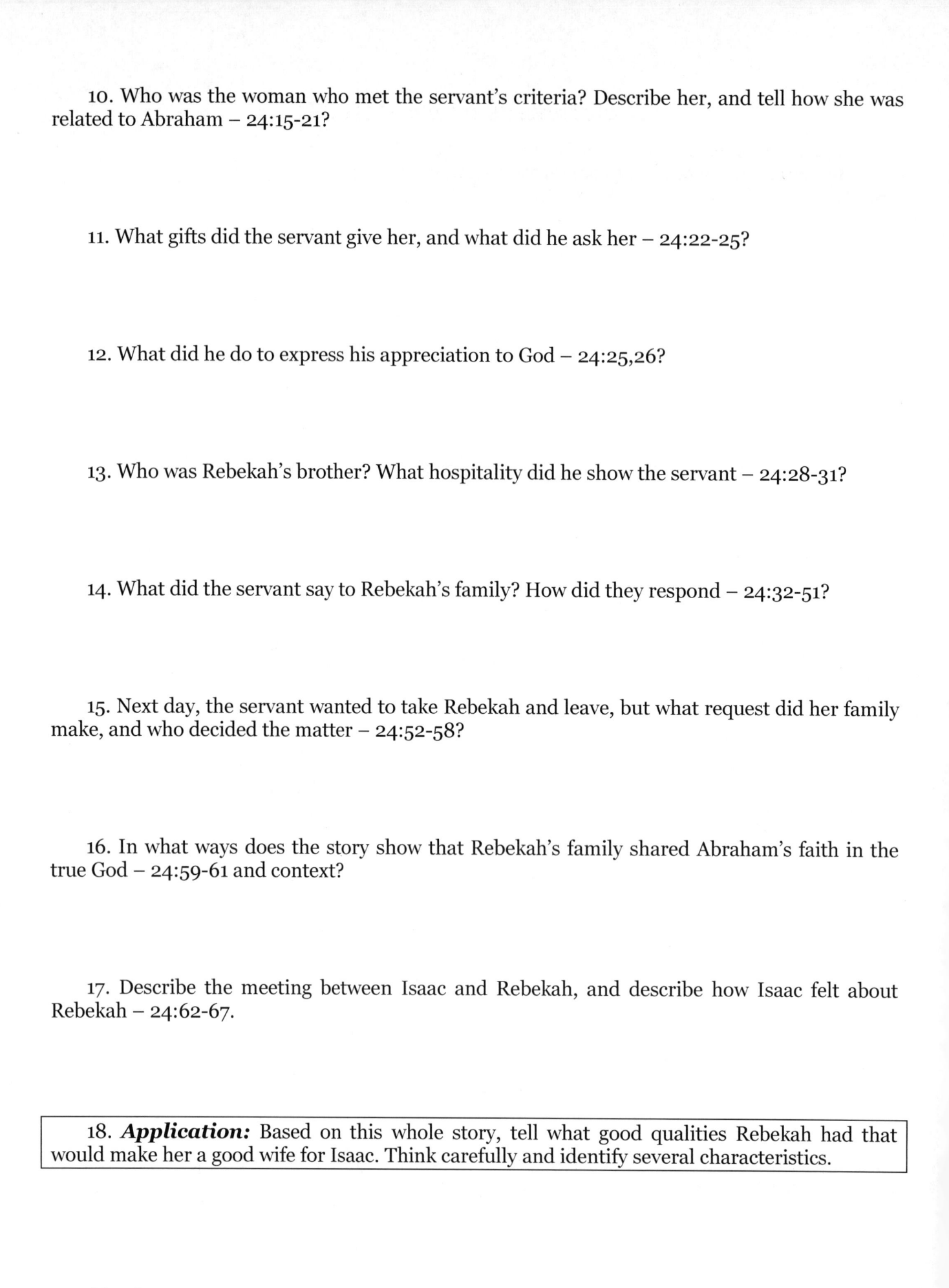

10. Who was the woman who met the servant's criteria? Describe her, and tell how she was related to Abraham – 24:15-21?

11. What gifts did the servant give her, and what did he ask her – 24:22-25?

12. What did he do to express his appreciation to God – 24:25,26?

13. Who was Rebekah's brother? What hospitality did he show the servant – 24:28-31?

14. What did the servant say to Rebekah's family? How did they respond – 24:32-51?

15. Next day, the servant wanted to take Rebekah and leave, but what request did her family make, and who decided the matter – 24:52-58?

16. In what ways does the story show that Rebekah's family shared Abraham's faith in the true God – 24:59-61 and context?

17. Describe the meeting between Isaac and Rebekah, and describe how Isaac felt about Rebekah – 24:62-67.

18. *Application:* Based on this whole story, tell what good qualities Rebekah had that would make her a good wife for Isaac. Think carefully and identify several characteristics.

Assignments on Genesis 25

Please read Genesis 25 and answer these questions:

1. After Sarah's death, whom did Abraham marry – 25:1-4? Name her sons.

2. **Special Assignment:** List the nations that descended from Abraham.

3. Who received Abraham's inheritance – 25:5,6? What about his other sons? (Think: Why?)

4. How old was Abraham when he died – 25:7-10? Who buried him and where?

5. How many sons did Ishmael have, and what passage does this fulfill – 25:12-16?

6. What problem did Isaac and Rebekah have that was similar to a problem Abraham and Sarah had – 25:19-21? Why would this be a special concern for them?

7. **Application:** When Rebekah conceived, "the children struggled within her" – 25:22. Where else are unborn children called "children," "babies," "infants," etc.? What are the consequences to abortion?

8. What prophecy did God make regarding the sons of Isaac and Rebekah – 25:23?

9. **Case Study:** Some say this proves God unconditionally predestines some individuals to be saved and others to be lost. Study other **passages** referring to this event and respond.

10. What were the sons named? What did the older son look like? What did the younger son do at birth – 25:24-26? (Think: What is the significance of the hand on the heel?)

11. What were the two boys like when they grew older and what preference did the parents have between the boys – 25:27,28?

12. **Application:** Should parents have favorite children? Explain.

13. What is a birthright? How did Jacob obtain the birthright – 25:29-34? (Think: Where does the New Testament refer to this event? What does this tell you about Esau and Jacob?)

Assignments on Genesis 26

Please read Genesis 26 and answer these questions:

1. Summarize what we know about Isaac prior to Genesis 26.

2. Where did Isaac move and why – 26:1,2?

3. What promises did God make to Isaac – 26:3-5? What is the significance?

4. Why did God give this promise – 26:5? (Think: Did Abraham keep the 10 Commands?)

5. **Special Assignment:** Make a list of **passages** in Genesis referring to these promises.

6. What falsehood did Isaac tell the men of Gerar – 26:7? Why?

7. Who discovered the truth, and how – 26:8-11? What did he do about it? (Think: What event does this remind you of?)

8. Describe Isaac's prosperity – 26:12-14. What effect did this have on the Philistines?

9. Describe the problems Isaac had with the Philistines as a result – 26:15-22? How did he deal with this? (Think: What lessons can we learn?)

10. Where did Isaac move next? What happened there – 26:23-25? (Think: What else do we know about this place?)

11. Describe how Isaac and Abimelech made peace 26:26-31. Where else do we read of a similar event?

12. Describe Esau's wives – 26:34,35. Why is this significant in subsequent events? (Think: How does this differ from the choice of a wife for Isaac? What can we learn?)

Workbook on Genesis

Assignments on Genesis 27

Please read Genesis 27 and answer these questions:

1. What request did Isaac make of Esau – 27:1-4? What did Isaac intend to do?

2. What is a "blessing" as described here? List and consider other **passages**.

3. What had God already revealed about Jacob and Esau's descendants? How did Isaac's conduct compare to God's intentions? (Think: How old were Esau and Jacob at this time? Boys?)

4. Describe Rebekah's plot – 27:5-10.

5. What subsequent events reveal she came from a deceitful family?

6. **Special Assignment:** Evaluate her plan. Was it right or wrong? Why?

7. Describe and evaluate Jacob's objection and Rebekah's response – 27:11-13.

8. What further arrangements did Rebekah make – 27:14-17?

9. What questions did Isaac ask Jacob, and how did he respond – 27:18-25?

10. **Special Assignment:** Discuss Jacob's treatment here of his father and his brother.

Page #43

Workbook on Genesis

11. Describe the blessing Isaac gave Jacob – 27:26-29.

12. Explain the fulfillment of this blessing. (Think: Did Isaac speak from his own ideas? Note 27:33,37. Explain.)

13. Tell what happened when Esau arrived – 27:30-33. Explain Heb. 12:17.

14. How did Isaac evaluate Jacob's conduct in 27:34-36?

15. Describe Isaac's blessing on Esau – 27:37-40. Explain.

16. What plot did Esau then devise – 27:41? What lessons can we learn?

17. How did Rebekah respond – 27:42-46? Did things work out as she hoped?

18. What arrangements did she make with Isaac?

19. Explain Hebrews 11:20 as compared to Genesis 27. Note Gen. 28:3,4.

20. **Application:** Why did God still give Jacob the promises of Abraham? Did He justify Jacob's conduct here? Can a man obtain God's favor by deceit? See also question #3 on this chapter and Gen. 45:5-11; 50:15-21; chap. 48,49.

Workbook on Genesis

Assignments on Genesis 28

Please read Genesis 28 and answer these questions:

1. Where did Jacob go to find a wife – 28:1,2? Why? What previous event was similar?

2. What blessing did Isaac pronounce on Jacob – 28:3,4? Explain the significance. (Think: What does this show about Isaac?)

3. What effect did this have on Esau, and what did he do about it – 28:6-9? (Think: Did this solve Esau's problem? Explain.)

4. What arrangement did Jacob make for his sleep – 28:11?

5. Describe Jacob's dream – 28:12-15.

6. What promises did God make to Jacob? Why was this important?

7. **Special Assignment:** Explain the meaning of the dream. Who are angels, and what is their purpose? Cf. John 1:51.

8. How did this affect Jacob, and what conclusion did he reach – 28:16,17?

9. What did he do with the stone – 28:18? What was the significance?

10. What name did he give the place – 28:19 (see *map*)? What did it mean?

11. What vow did Jacob make – 28:20-22? What is a vow? (Think: What significance would this event have in Jacob's life?)

12. **Special Assignment:** What is tithing? What does the Bible say about it? Does the New Testament teach it? Explain.

Assignments on Genesis 29

Please read Genesis 29 and answer these questions:
1. Where did Jacob go when he arrived? What was happening? Why – 29:1-3?

---

2. **Special Assignment:** Note similarities to how a wife was found for Isaac.

---

3. About whom did Jacob inquire, and what did the people answer – 29:4-6?

4. What explanation did the men give about watering the flocks – 29:7,8?

5. Whom did Jacob meet at the well, and how did he greet her – 29:9-11?

6. What did he tell her and what did she do – 29:12?

7. How did Laban greet Jacob – 29:13,14?

8. Describe Laban's two daughters – 29:16,17.

9. What agreement did Jacob make with Laban – 29:15-19? Why?

10. How does this compare to the selection of Rebekah for Isaac?

Workbook on Genesis

11. Describe Jacob's love for Rachel – 29:20.

12. What can we learn about weddings from this story?

13. When the wedding occurred, how did Laban deceive Jacob – 29:21-26? (Think: Why didn't Jacob realize he had the wrong woman?)

14. What did Jacob say to Laban about this – 29:25? (Think: Jacob had earlier practiced deceit. What lessons was he learning about it now?)

15. How did Laban explain his conduct – 29:26,27? (Think: Was this a good answer? What do we learn about deceit in Rebekah's family?)

16. **Application:** Evaluate the conduct of Laban, Rachel, and Leah in this. Who was right or wrong? Why?

17. What agreement was reached then – 29:27-30?

18. What problems did this arrangement lead to?

19. **Application:** Who else practiced favoritism? What lessons can we learn? What can we learn about polygamy?

20. Which of Jacob's wives had children first – 29:31? Why?

21. Name her first four sons and define their names – 29:32-35.

Assignments on Genesis 30

Please read Genesis 30 and answer these questions:

1. How did Rachel feel about being barren – 30:1? What did she say?

2. How did Jacob respond – 30:2?

> 3. **Special Assignment:** Why was childbearing important to these women? Are children a blessing today?

4. What solution did Rachel propose – 30:3?

5. Describe who else had earlier used a similar approach and what happened as a result.

6. Name the sons born as a result – 30:4-8. What did their names mean?

7. Who also called in a "pinch-hitter" – 30:9? Whom did Jacob then marry?

8. Name the sons born and define their names – 30:10-13.

9. What bargain did Leah and Rachel make – 30:14,15?

10. What irony do you see in Leah's accusation that **Rachel** had taken **her** husband?

11. What happened as a result? Name the son born and define the name – 30:16-18.

Workbook on Genesis

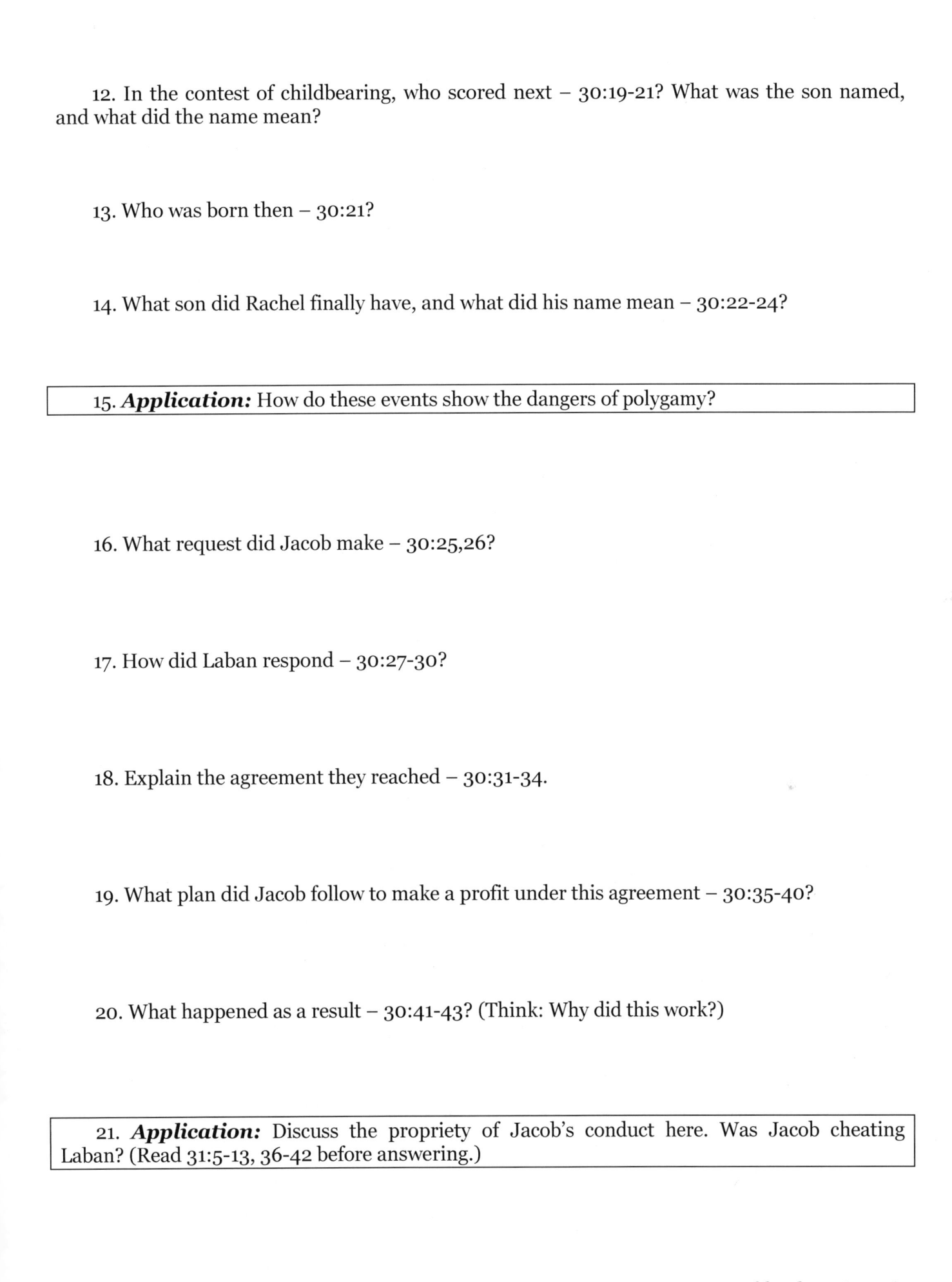

12. In the contest of childbearing, who scored next – 30:19-21? What was the son named, and what did the name mean?

13. Who was born then – 30:21?

14. What son did Rachel finally have, and what did his name mean – 30:22-24?

15. **Application:** How do these events show the dangers of polygamy?

16. What request did Jacob make – 30:25,26?

17. How did Laban respond – 30:27-30?

18. Explain the agreement they reached – 30:31-34.

19. What plan did Jacob follow to make a profit under this agreement – 30:35-40?

20. What happened as a result – 30:41-43? (Think: Why did this work?)

21. **Application:** Discuss the propriety of Jacob's conduct here. Was Jacob cheating Laban? (Read 31:5-13, 36-42 before answering.)

Page #49   *Workbook on Genesis*

Assignments on Genesis 31

Please read Genesis 31 and answer these questions:

1. What did Jacob perceive regarding Laban and his sons – 31:1,2?

2. What did God tell him to do – 31:3?

3. With whom did Jacob discuss the situation? How did he describe Laban's treatment of him and his treatment of Laban – 31:4-7?

4. What explanation did Jacob give for why the flocks conceived as they did – 31:5-9? Who gave the animals to him?

5. How did Jacob know God was responsible for the way the animals reproduced – 31:10-13? (Think: Was Jacob deceitful in how these animals reproduced?)

6. What conclusion did Rachel and Leah reach – 31:14-16? Why?

7. Describe how Jacob's family left – 31:17-20.

8. In what direction did they travel – 31:21 (see a *map*)?

9. What sin did Rachel commit? What does this show about her family?

10. **Application:** Give examples of people today who claim to worship the true God but also participate in sinful practices like people around them.

Workbook on Genesis

11. When did Laban learn that Jacob had left? What did he do – 31:22,23?

12. What warning did God give – 31:24? (Think: What does this show about Laban?)

13. What questions did Laban ask Jacob when he caught him – 31:25-27?

14. What did he say he would have done had he known they were leaving – 31:28? (Think: Does this explanation harmonize with his character and past conduct?)

15. What reasons did Jacob give for leaving secretly – 31:31?

16. What did he say about Laban's gods – 31:32?

17. How did Rachel escape detection – 31:33-35?

18. Summarize Jacob's speech in 31:36-42.

19. What does this speech show about Jacob's service to Laban? What does it show about his attitude toward deceit?

20. What proposal did Laban make, and what happened as a result – 31:43,44?

21. What was the significance of the stones? What names were they given – 31:45-52?

22. How did Jacob and Laban separate – 31:53-55?

Assignments on Genesis 32

Please read Genesis 32 and answer these questions:

1. What happened as Jacob continued his journey? What did he name the place, and what does the name mean – 32:1,2? (Think: Explain the significance of this event.)

2. To whom did Jacob send messengers, and what was the message – 32:3-5? Where did Esau live (see *map*)?

3. What news did the men bring in return? How did this affect Jacob, and what did he do – 32:6-8? (Think: Why would this news distress Jacob so?)

4. Summarize Jacob's prayer – 32:9-12. What was his request, and on what did he base it?

5. Describe his gift for Esau – 32:13-15. What was the purpose of the gift (cf. v20)?

6. How were the gifts sent, and what did the messengers say – 32:16-21?

7. Where was Jacob at this time – 32:22? Locate on a *map*.

8. What conflict did Jacob face that night? What injury did he receive – 32:24,25?

9. Where else is this event mentioned? What information does this add?

10. What request did Jacob make? What change was made in his name, and what is the significance – 32:26-28?

11. **Special Assignment:** Explain the purpose of this event. In what sense had Jacob struggled with God and man? (Consider the situation and Jacob's prayer.)

12. What did Jacob name the place where this occurred? What does this mean? Locate it on a *map* – 32:20-31. (Think: In what sense had Jacob seen God's face? Cf. other passages.)

13. How did Jacob's descendants memorialize this event – 32:32?

Workbook on Genesis

Assignments on Genesis 33

Please read Genesis 33 and answer these questions:

1. In what order did Jacob's family meet Esau – 33:1-3? (Think: Why choose this order?)

2. Describe the meeting of Jacob and Esau – 33:4. What conclusions can be reached and what lessons learned?

3. **Special Assignment:** Based on what we have learned, discuss why this would have been such an emotional event.

4. How did Jacob describe his children, and how did his family act toward Esau – 33:5-7? What can we learn?

5. What did Jacob say was the purpose of his gifts to Esau – 33:8-11?

6. What discussion followed about the gifts, and what was the end result – 33:9-11?

7. How did Esau suggest they proceed? How did Jacob respond, and why – 33:12-14?

8. What did Esau suggest next, and what was the result – 33:15,16? (Think: What does this discussion imply about Jacob and Esau's attitudes?)

9. Where did Jacob go next? What did he do there – 33:17?

10. What did he name this place? (Think: What does this name mean, and where is the place located? See *map*.)

11. Where did Jacob go next, and where is it located – 33:18 (see *map*)?

12. What two things did he do there – 33:19,20? (Think: Where else have such things happened?)

Assignments on Genesis 34

Please read Genesis 34 and answer these questions:
1. Where did Jacob's daughter go – 34:1?

2. Whom did she meet there, and what sin occurred – 34:2?

3. List other *passages* about sexual union between unmarried people.

4. **Application:** What can we learn about the problems of keeping children pure in an immoral society?

5. What did Shechem want to do afterward? Why – 34:3,4?

6. Contrast the reaction of Shechem's family to the reaction of Dinah's family – 34:5-7. (Think: What does this show about the morals of that society?)

7. What proposition did Hamor present to Jacob and his sons – 34:8-11? (Think: How would such a proposal have impressed Jacob's family, especially under the circumstances?)

8. What request and proposal did Shechem make – 34:12?

9. What answer did Jacob's sons give – 34:13-17?

10. What troubling family trait showed itself in Jacob's sons' answer?

Workbook on Genesis

11. How did Hamor and Shechem present this proposed arrangement to the men of the land – 34:18-23?

12. How did their proposal to the men of the land differ from what they had proposed to Jacob's sons? What does this tell you?

13. What does 34:19 tell about Shechem? What does this in turn show about the other men?

14. What did the men of the land do – 34:24?

15. What did Jacob's two sons do to the men of the city? Which two did it – 34:24-26?

16. What did Jacobs' sons do then – 34:27-29?

17. What did Jacob say about this to his sons – 34:30?

18. How did they reply – 34:31?

19. What was later done to Simeon and Levi because of this (49:5-7)?

20. *Application:* What was right or wrong about the sons' deed? What responsibility did Jacob bear in it?

Assignments on Genesis 35

Please read Genesis 35 and answer these questions:

1. What instructions did God give – 35:1? What else had happened at Bethel?

2. What did Jacob tell his family – 35:2-4? What does this tell you?

3. **Special Assignment:** How would God's instructions relate to recent events? What lessons can we learn about the impact society can have on our families?

4. How did the people of the land treat them – 35:5? Why?

5. Who died – 35:8? Where else have we read of her? Where was she buried? (Think: What does this show about the importance of servants?)

6. What did God do at Bethel this time – 35:9-12? (Think: What does this show about Jacob's relationship to God?)

7. What did Jacob do in response to God – 35:14,15?

8. Describe the birth of Jacob's last son. What was he named (define) – 35:16-19?

9. What happened to Rachel? Where did this occur– 35:19,20?

10. What sin did Reuben commit – 35:22? (Think: Should Reuben have known better?)

11. What punishment did Reuben receive (see cross-references)?

12. Summarize Jacob's wives and sons – 35:23-26.

13. Where did Jacob see his father again? (See *map*.) Describe Isaac's death– 35:27-29.

14. **Application:** What can we learn from the sins and evil we have seen in Jacob's family?

Workbook on Genesis

Assignments on Genesis 36

Please read Genesis 36 and answer these questions:

1. Summarize the theme of Genesis 36. Where else is such a genealogy found?

2. What was Esau's other name – 36:1, and where else do we read about it?

3. What promise had been given to Esau (27:39,40)? How does this chapter relate to the fulfillment of that promise?

4. Name Esau's wives – 36:2,3.

5. Name Esau's five sons – 36:4,5.

6. Where did Esau move – 36:6-8? Why? (Think: What does this tell you about Jacob and Esau? Where else have we read of a similar event?)

7. Describe the location of the area that Esau moved to. (See **map**.)

8. What was the name of the concubine of Esau's son Eliphaz – 36:12? What was her son's name? (Think: What significance does a nation with this name have in later Bible history?)

9. Whose descendants are recorded beginning in – 36:20? What is his significance?

10. What information is given beginning in – 36:31?

11. **Special Assignment:** Summarize the nations we have now learned who have descended from Abraham.

Assignments on Genesis 37

Please read Genesis 37 and answer these questions.

1. How old was Joseph? What job did he have – 37:2? (Think: Who else in the Bible had a similar job?)

2. **Application:** What lessons can we learn from Joseph's age in this study?

3. What did Joseph do in 37:2 that would have angered his brothers?

4. How did Jacob feel about Joseph, and how did he show this feeling – 37:3,4? How did Joseph's brothers react?

5. List and discuss another example of parents who played favorites with their children.

6. **Application:** What problems can be caused when parents show favoritism?

7. Describe Joseph's first dream and explain its meaning – 37:5-8. (Think: What are sheaves?)

8. Describe his second dream and explain what it meant – 37:9,10.

Workbook on Genesis

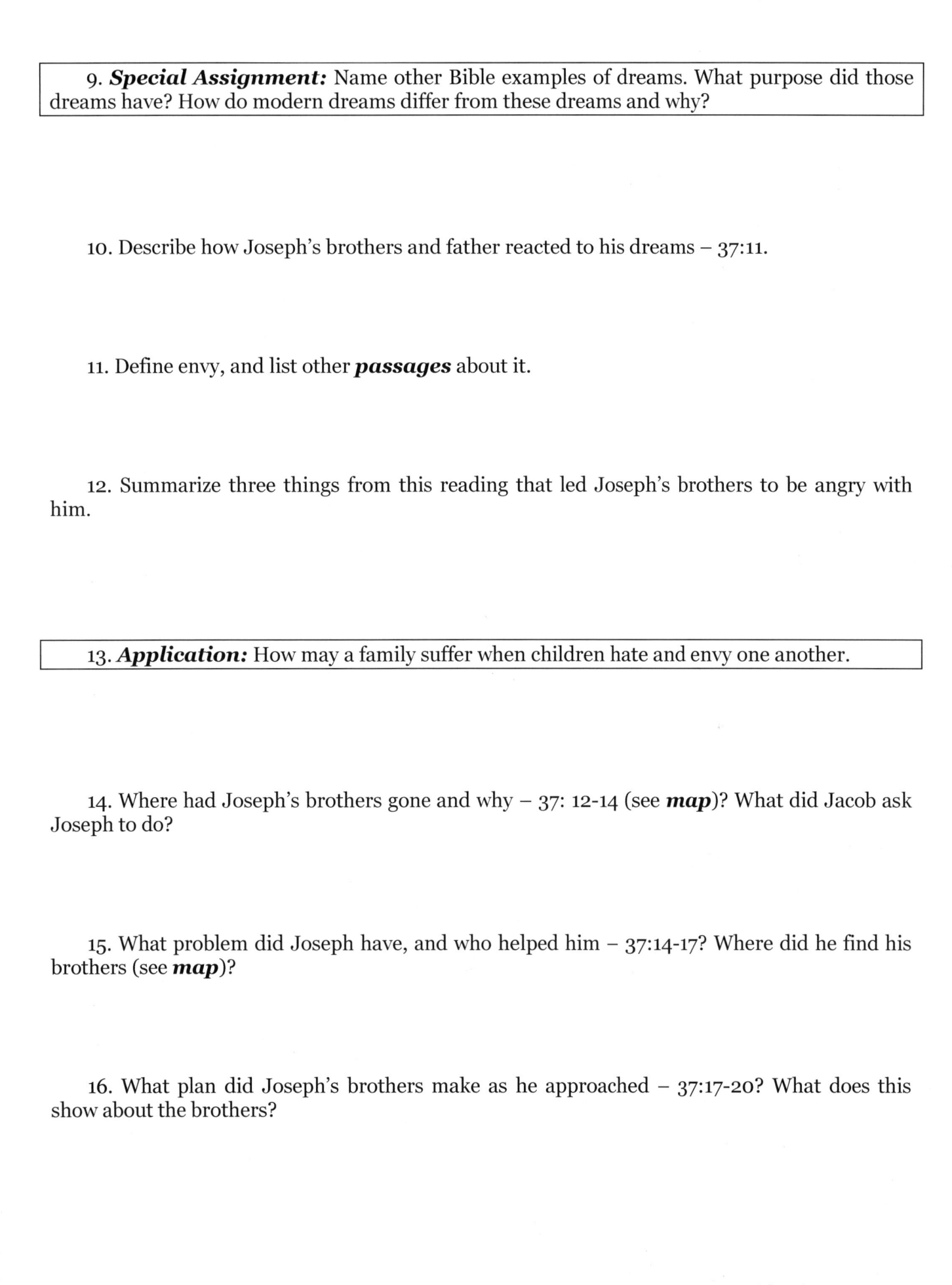

9. **Special Assignment:** Name other Bible examples of dreams. What purpose did those dreams have? How do modern dreams differ from these dreams and why?

10. Describe how Joseph's brothers and father reacted to his dreams – 37:11.

11. Define envy, and list other **passages** about it.

12. Summarize three things from this reading that led Joseph's brothers to be angry with him.

13. **Application:** How may a family suffer when children hate and envy one another.

14. Where had Joseph's brothers gone and why – 37: 12-14 (see **map**)? What did Jacob ask Joseph to do?

15. What problem did Joseph have, and who helped him – 37:14-17? Where did he find his brothers (see **map**)?

16. What plan did Joseph's brothers make as he approached – 37:17-20? What does this show about the brothers?

Page #59   Workbook on Genesis

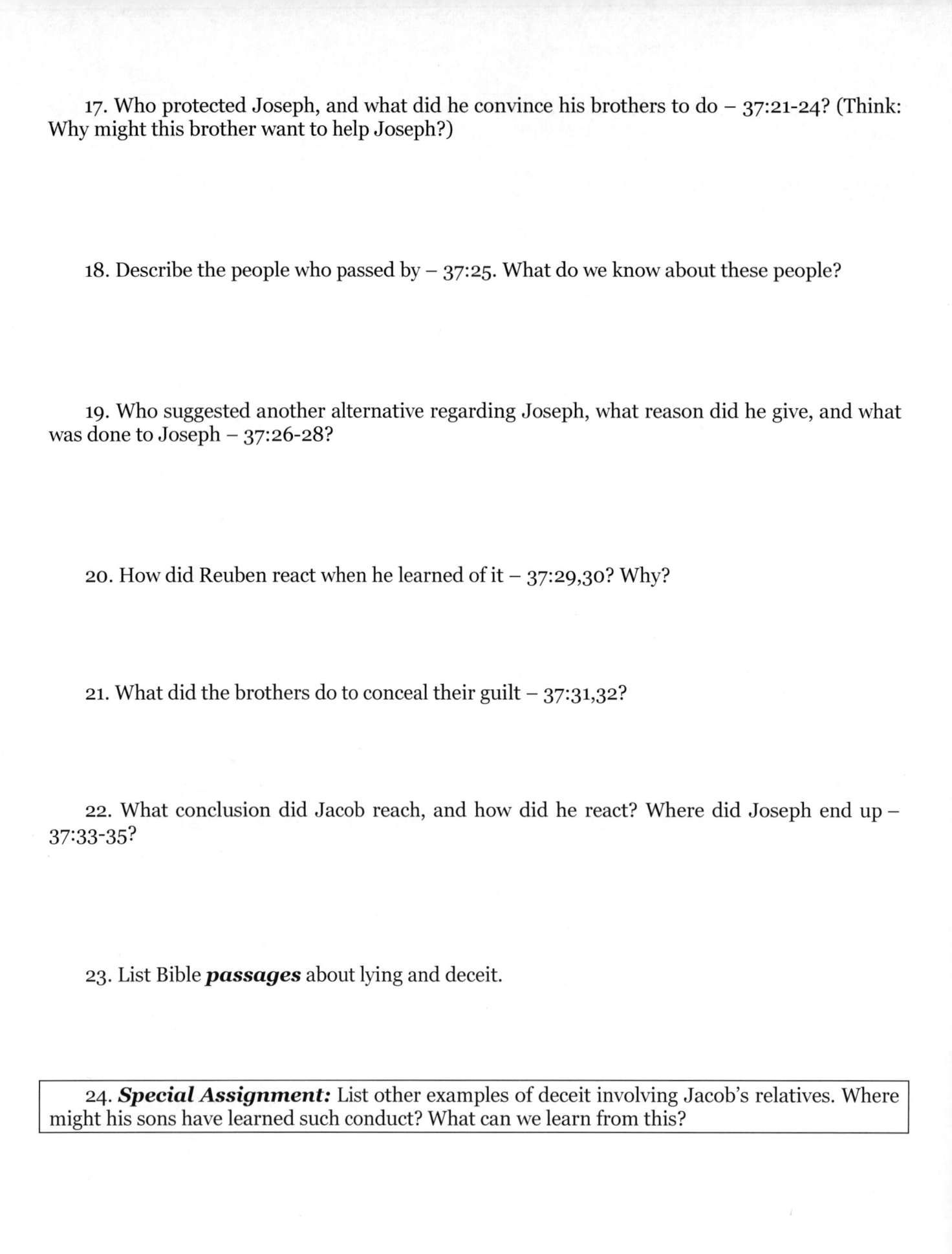

17. Who protected Joseph, and what did he convince his brothers to do – 37:21-24? (Think: Why might this brother want to help Joseph?)

18. Describe the people who passed by – 37:25. What do we know about these people?

19. Who suggested another alternative regarding Joseph, what reason did he give, and what was done to Joseph – 37:26-28?

20. How did Reuben react when he learned of it – 37:29,30? Why?

21. What did the brothers do to conceal their guilt – 37:31,32?

22. What conclusion did Jacob reach, and how did he react? Where did Joseph end up – 37:33-35?

23. List Bible *passages* about lying and deceit.

24. **Special Assignment:** List other examples of deceit involving Jacob's relatives. Where might his sons have learned such conduct? What can we learn from this?

Workbook on Genesis

Assignments on Genesis 38

Please read Genesis 38, then answer the following questions:

1. **Special Assignment:** Read chapter 38. As you study the chapter, consider why God would record these events about Judah. What benefit is this material to us?

2. Whom did Judah visit? Whom did he marry – 38:1,2? (Think: What may be observed about his choice of wife?)

3. Name his 3 sons. Where did he live at the time – 38:3-5?

4. Whom did Judah's first son marry – 38:6?

5. What happened to Judah's first son, and why – 38:7? (Think: Explain this in light of the evil in Jacob's family.)

6. What was the next son told to do – 38:8? Why?

7. **Special Assignment:** Find verses about the law involved in this story. Explain it.

8. What sin did Onan commit? What happened to him – 38:9,10?

9. **Case Study:** Catholicism says Onan's case proves contraceptives are sinful. How would you respond?

10. What promise did Judah make to Tamar – 38:11?

11. Who else died – 38:12? Where did Judah go?

Page #61   *Workbook on Genesis*

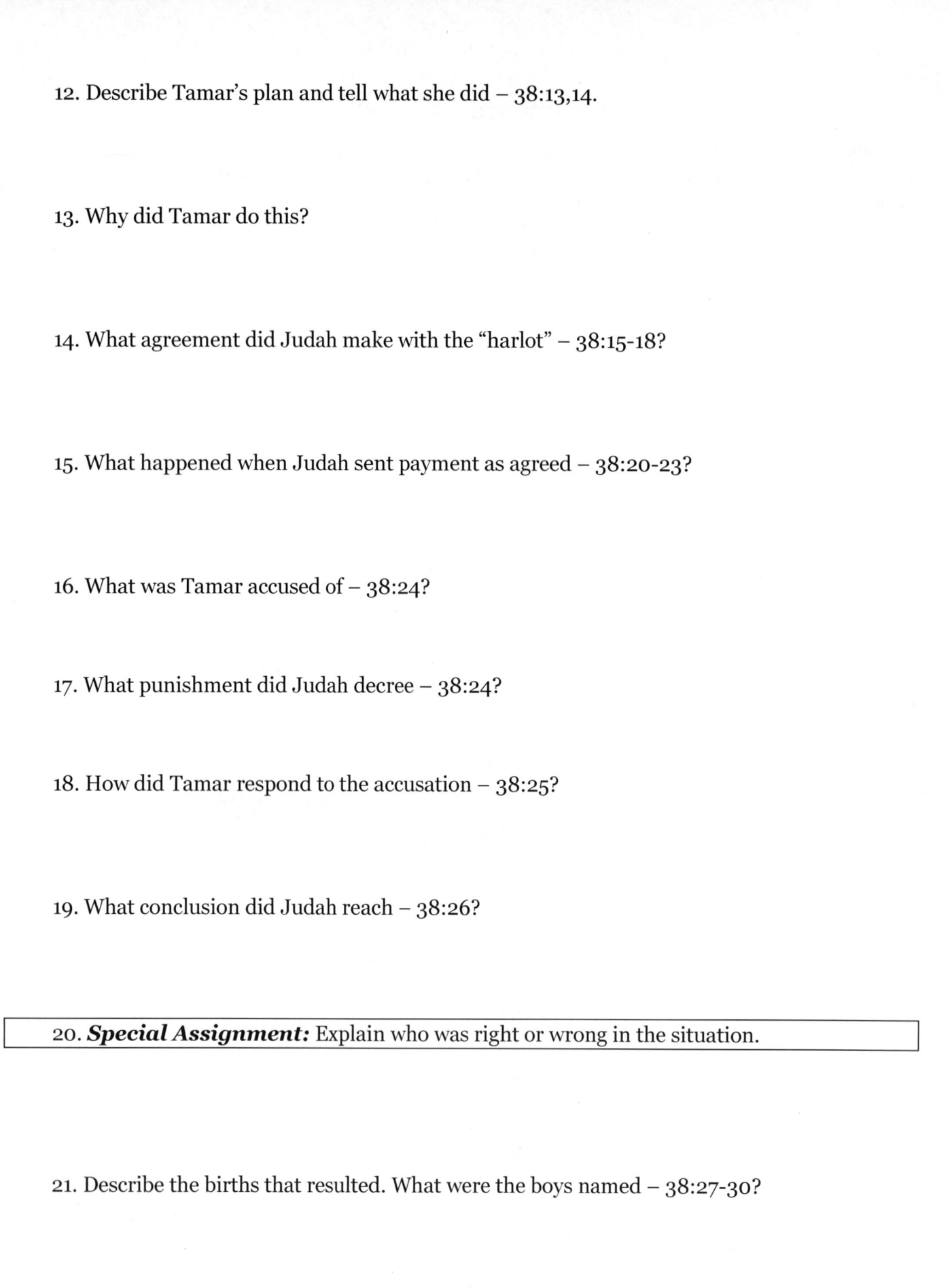

12. Describe Tamar's plan and tell what she did – 38:13,14.

13. Why did Tamar do this?

14. What agreement did Judah make with the "harlot" – 38:15-18?

15. What happened when Judah sent payment as agreed – 38:20-23?

16. What was Tamar accused of – 38:24?

17. What punishment did Judah decree – 38:24?

18. How did Tamar respond to the accusation – 38:25?

19. What conclusion did Judah reach – 38:26?

> 20. **Special Assignment:** Explain who was right or wrong in the situation.

21. Describe the births that resulted. What were the boys named – 38:27-30?

Workbook on Genesis   Page #62

Assignments on Genesis 39

Please read Genesis 39, then answer the following questions:

1. In whose house did Joseph serve, and what position did this man have – 39:1?

2. Describe the treatment Joseph received in this man's house, both by God and by his master – 39:2-6? (Think: In what sense was the Lord with Joseph?)

3. Who tempted Joseph, and what did she want to do – 39:7? (Think: Why would this be tempting to Joseph?)

4. **Application:** Describe two reasons Joseph gave for refusing – 39:8,9. What does this teach us about the proper motives for our lives?

5. How did Potiphar's wife react to Joseph's refusal? What did he do about it – 39:10?

6. What final effort did she make to tempt him, and how did he react – 39:11,12? (Think: Contrast Joseph's actions to those of other people in his family in the face of temptation.)

7. **Application:** What lessons can we learn about handling temptation? Give b/c/v for other relevant passages.

8. Describe what Potiphar's wife said had happened – 39:16-18.

9. List other **passages** showing how evil people sometimes mistreat good people. (Think: Why do evil people do these things?)

10. What did Potiphar do to Joseph, and what happened to him there – 39:19-23? (Think: What does Joseph's conduct teach us?)

11. **Define** "providence." As the story of Joseph proceeds, make a list of whatever lessons you can learn about providence.

Assignments on Genesis 40

Please read Genesis 40, then answer the following questions:

1. Describe the problem two of the king's officers faced – 40:1-3.

2. How did these officers come in contact with Joseph – 40:3,4?

3. Why were the officers sad when Joseph found them one morning – 40:5-8?

4. What did Joseph explain regarding interpretation of dreams – 40:8? (Note: Review our discussion of dreams from Gen. 37.)

5. Describe the butler's dream – 40:9-11. (Think: What was the butler's job? Why was it important?)

6. What was the interpretation of his dream – 40:12,13?

7. What request did Joseph make after interpreting the dream – 40:14,15? (Think: What role did this request ultimately play in Joseph's life?)

8. Describe the baker's dream – 40:16,17.

9. What was the interpretation of this dream – 40:18,19? (Think: In the dream, had the baker protected the bread as he should? What might this indicate?)

10. Tell how the dreams were fulfilled – 40:20-23. (Think: Did the butler fulfill Joseph's request?)

Workbook on Genesis

Assignments on Genesis 41

Please read Genesis 41, then answer the following questions:
1. Describe Pharaoh's first dream – 41:1-4.

2. Describe his second dream – 41:5-7.

3. Whom did he ask to interpret the dreams? What happened – 41:8?

4. *Application:* What does this prove about magicians and the occult?

5. Explain how Pharaoh found an interpreter – 41:9-13.

6. *Special Assignment:* How had the dreams of the butler and baker helped those men? What was the real reason why God sent those dreams?

7. How did Joseph prepare for his audience with Pharaoh – 41:14? (Think: Why did he do this, and what can we learn? Did people in Bible times know how to cut hair?)

8. What explanation did Joseph give Pharaoh about interpretation of dreams – 41:15?

9. What does Joseph's explanation teach about God's power – 41:16? Did Joseph take glory to himself? What should we learn?

10. Explain – 41:25. What is meant by "the dream is one"? What was the purpose of the dreams? Why had the dream been repeated?

11. Explain the meaning of Pharaoh's dreams – 41:25-32.

12. What advice did Joseph give Pharaoh – 41:33-36?

13. How did Pharaoh then view Joseph – 41:37-39?

14. Describe the position Joseph was given – 41:40-44.

15. Describe the honors Joseph received – 41:42-44. What is the significance? (Think: Consider the incredible changes that occurred in Joseph's life in just one day.)

16. What name was Joseph given, and whom did he marry – 41:45? (Think: What was Pharaoh's purpose in these decisions?)

17. How old was Joseph at this time – 41:46? How long had he been in Egypt?

18. What preparations did Joseph make during the years of plenty? How much food was gathered – 41:47-49? (Think: Why was this a wise plan?)

19. What children did Joseph have and what did he name them – 41:50-52?

20. Describe the famine. How bad was it – 41:53-56?

21. **Special Assignment:** Which came first for Joseph: a period of trial or a period of blessing? What lesson should we learn?

22. **Special Assignment:** How does this show God's providence? Explain the evidence that God's providence was working even while Joseph was suffering.

Workbook on Genesis

Assignments on Genesis 42

Please read Genesis 42, then answer the following questions:

1. What did Jacob tell his sons to do, and why – 42:1-4? Why didn't Benjamin go?

2. When the brothers bought grain, what prediction did they fulfill – 42:5-8? (Think: Why did Joseph recognize his brothers, but not vice versa?)

3. How did Joseph treat his brothers, and what accusation did he make – 42:9-16? (Think: How long had it been since Joseph had seen his brothers? Proof?)

4. What information did the brothers give about their family?

5. What did Joseph do to them – 42:17?

6. What course of action did he finally settle on – 42:18-20? (Think: What reasons did Joseph have for all this? Vengeance?)

> 7. **Special Assignment:** List and explain Bible **passages** about repentance.

8. What did the brothers confess? How did Reuben explain the situation – 42:21,22? (Think: Why would they say this, since they did not recognize Joseph?)

9. How was Joseph affected by this discussion – 42:23,24?

10. Who stayed in Egypt? What did Joseph do for the other brothers – 42:25-28? (Think: How did this affect the brothers?)

11. Summarize the report Jacob's sons brought to him – 42:29-34.

12. What did the brothers discover? How did this affect them and Jacob – 42:35?

13. What did Jacob say about the plan to take Benjamin to Egypt? Why – 42:36?

14. How did Reuben try to reassure Jacob – 42:37,38?

Assignments on Genesis 43

Please read Genesis 43, then answer the following questions:
1. What did Jacob request? Why? Who responded, and what did he say – 43:1-5?

2. What complaint did Jacob raise, and how did the brothers respond – 43:6,7?

3. What assurance did Judah give Jacob? What reason did he give – 43:8-10? (Think: What qualities is Judah beginning to demonstrate?)

4. What decision did Jacob make, and what advice did he give – 43:11-15? (Think: What does this show about the famine in Canaan?)

5. Explain 43:14 in your own words.

6. What did Joseph invite his brothers to do, and what did they think – 43:16-18?

7. What did they tell the steward? How did he answer – 43:19-23? Explain the answer.

8. Who joined them, and how did they prepare to meet Joseph – 43:23-26?

9. What was Joseph's first question, and how did they respond – 43:27,28?

10. What did he say to Benjamin, and how did he react to meeting him – 43:29,30?

11. Explain the seating – 43:31,32. (Think: What did this show about Joseph's position?)

12. **Special Assignment:** Summarize what the Bible teaches about the superiority of races and nationalities.

13. Explain the seating of Joseph's brothers and how this affected them – 43:33.

14. How did Benjamin's meal differ from that of his brothers – 43:34? (Think: Consider how Joseph's conduct would affect his brothers.)

Workbook on Genesis

Assignments on Genesis 44

Please read Genesis 44, then answer the following questions:
1. What instructions did Joseph give his servant in 44:1,2?

2. What accusation did the steward make against the men – 44:3-6? (Think: Define "divining." Did Joseph actually divine? What was the source of his power?)

3. What response did the brothers give to the accusation – 44:7-9?

4. What consequences did the servant say he would demand – 44:10?

5. Who was considered guilty, and what did the brothers do – 44:11-13?

6. What did Judah confess? What punishment did Joseph require – 44:14-17?

7. **Special Assignment:** Explain what Joseph was trying to accomplish? Explain the similarities between his own situation and the one he had set up for Benjamin.

8. Summarize the story as Judah told it – 44:18-29.

9. What problem did Judah fear – 44:30,31?

10. Why did Judah feel especially responsible for Benjamin?

11. What alternative did Judah propose, and what reason did he give – 44:33,34? (Think: Note the similarities between Jesus' sacrifice and what Judah proposed.)

12. **Special Assignment:** Summarize how Judah's statement showed repentance.

Assignments on Genesis 45

Please read Genesis 45, then answer the following questions:
1. How was Joseph affected by Judah's speech, and what did he do – 45:1,2?

2. What did he tell his brothers, and how did they react – 45:3? (Think: Why would they react this way? How would they feel?)

3. Was Joseph angry with his brothers? What was his explanation for what had happened – 45:4-8? (Think: Did Joseph mean his brothers were not responsible for their conduct? Explain.)

4. **Special Assignment:** Explain how 45:5-8 gives a good explanation of providence.

5. What did Joseph say the brothers should do next – 45:9-13? Why? (Think: What does all this show regarding how thoroughly Joseph had thought out this situation?)

6. Where did Joseph say his family could live (see **map**)?

7. How did he then greet the brothers – 45:14,15?

8. Who heard about Joseph's brothers, and what did he say to do – 45:16-20?

9. Summarize what Joseph gave his brothers – 45:21-24. (Think: Explain v24.)

10. What did Jacob first think when his sons told him the news – 45:25,26?

11. What convinced Jacob, and what did he conclude – 45:27,28? (Think: How would all this affect Jacob?)

12. **Special Assignment:** Summarize the lessons this story teaches about forgiveness.

Workbook on Genesis

Assignments on Genesis 46

Please read Genesis 46, then answer the following questions:

1. Where did Israel stop in his journey (see **map**), and what did he do there – 46:1? (Think: To whom had God previously made a promise at this place?)

2. What did God promise Jacob – 46:2-4? (Think: How would this help Jacob?)

> 3. **Special Assignment:** List other **passages** that refer to these promises.

4. Describe who and what Jacob took to Egypt – 46:5-7.

5. List the sons and daughter of Leah. Name Levi's sons – 46:8-25. (Think: Why are Levi's sons especially significant?)

6. Name the sons of the following:
   Of Zilpah:

   Of Rachel

   Of Bilhah

7. How many altogether went to Egypt – 46:26,27.

8. Who preceded Jacob? Why – 46:28?

9. Into what land did they move?

10. Who went to meet Jacob? Describe the meeting – 46:29,30.

11. Whom did Joseph want to tell about his family's arrival? What were the brothers to say was their occupation? Why – 46:31-34?

> 12. **Special Assignment:** Which of Jacob's ancestors had been herdsmen?

Workbook on Genesis

Assignments on Genesis 47

Please read Genesis 47, then answer the following questions:

1. To whom did Joseph present some of his brothers, and what request did they make – 47:1-4? (Think: Could Joseph have decided this himself? Why do it this way?)

2. What decision did Pharaoh make about arrangements for Joseph's family – 47:5,6?

3. What work did Pharaoh request Josephs' family to do for him?

4. What did Jacob do for Pharaoh – 47:7? (Think: What does this show about Jacob and Pharaoh — see Hebrews 7:7?)

5. What did Pharaoh ask Jacob, and what did Jacob answer – 47:8,9?

6. *Special Assignment:* How would the arrangement, as described in 47:11,12, fit God's promise to Abraham and the overall plan of the Bible?

7. What did the people do at first to obtain grain – 47:13,14?

8. *Special Assignment:* Was this arrangement fair or unfair? Explain.

9. What did the people do next to obtain grain – 47:15-17?

10. *Case Study:* Why did Joseph not institute a system of government welfare to care for the people? What can we learn about government welfare?

Workbook on Genesis

11. How did the people next obtain grain – 47:18-20? Whose idea was this?

12. Where did Joseph put the Egyptian people – 47:21?

13. Whose land was not taken? Why not – 47:22?

14. What arrangement did Joseph establish with the people in 47:23-26? How did the people react?

15. *Case Study:* Suppose someone says that Joseph was cruel to take the people's possessions and make them servants. How would you respond?

16. *Application:* What lessons can be learned from the story about slavery? Is slavery always cruel and unloving?

17. *Special Assignment:* Compare the tax rate these people paid to our taxes today. Was their tax burden unreasonable compared to ours?

18. How long did Jacob live in Egypt? How old was he when he died – 47:27,28?

19. What promise did Jacob require Joseph to make – 47:29-31?

20. Research Jacob's burial place, and explain what you can learn about it.

Assignments on Genesis 48

Please read Genesis 48, then answer the following questions:
1. Why did Joseph visit Jacob, and whom did he take with him – 48:1,2?

2. What promise did Jacob say God had given him – 48:3,4? Where else is this promise recorded? (Think: What is another name for Luz? See **map**.)

3. Explain again the significance of this promise in our study. (Think: Why was Jacob repeating this to Joseph?)

4. What promise did Jacob make regarding Joseph's sons in 48:5?

5. **Special Assignment:** Study parallel passages and explain the significance of Jacob's statement. See vv 16,22; Josh. 14:4; 1 Chron. 5:1.

6. What sad event did Jacob recall in 48:7, and where and when did it occur?

7. What did Jacob do to Joseph's sons? What observation did he make – 48:8-11?

8. What blessing did Jacob pronounce on the boys – 48:12-16? (Think: How does this relate to v5?)

9. Describe how Jacob placed his hands on the sons – 48:17,18. What did Joseph say?

10. What was the significance of where Jacob placed his hands? What were the consequences to the sons – 48:19,20?

11. What assurance did Jacob have regarding his family after he died – 48:21? (Think: How does v22 relate to v5?)

Workbook on Genesis

Assignments on Genesis 49

Please read Genesis 49, then answer the following questions:

1. Summarize what chap. 49 is about. (Think: Do Jacob's statements relate to his sons or to their descendants? Proof? Note v28.)

2. What did Jacob say regarding Reuben – 49:3,4? What event is referred to here? (Think: Where else have men pronounced blessings on their sons?)

3. What had Simeon and Levi done – 49:5-7? What did Jacob say about it?

4. Describe Jacob's prophecy about Judah – 49:8-12. Compare it to previous sons.

5. **Special Assignment:** What does 49:10 show about the tribe of Judah? (Think: Who/what is Shiloh?)

6. Summarize the statements regarding each of the following sons:
   Zebulun —

   Issachar —

   Dan —

   Gad —

   Asher —

   Naphtali —

7. What blessings are pronounced on Joseph – 49: 22-26 (note cross-references)?

8. Summarize the blessing on Benjamin – 49:27.

9. Explain how 49:28 shows the importance of all Jacob had just said. (Think: How do these statements relate to God's promises to Abraham?)

10. Where did Jacob want to be buried – 49:29-32? Describe his death.

Workbook on Genesis

Assignments on Genesis 50

Please read Genesis 50, then answer the following questions:

1. What did the physicians do with Jacob's body? How long did it take? How long did the Egyptians mourn for him – 50:1-3?

2. What request did Joseph then make? Why – 50:4-6?

3. Who went with Joseph? Who/what did not go – 50:7-9? (Think: What is indicated by the fact all these people went?)

4. Where did they stop and why – 50:10? How did this affect the Canaanites?

5. What name was given to this place, and what does the name mean?

6. What did the sons do with Jacob's body? What promise did this fulfill – 50:12,13?

7. What concern did Joseph's brothers have? What did they do about it – 50:14-18?

8. **Special Assignment:** What does the Bible teach about confessing sin and asking forgiveness of those whom we have wronged? Give *b/c/v*.

9. How did Joseph respond to his brothers? How did he say he would treat them – 50:19-21? (Think: Review what this teaches about forgiveness and God's providence.)

10. What are we told about the rest of Joseph's life – 50:22,23?

11. What promise did he ask his relatives to make regarding his body – 50:22-26? Where else does the Bible refer to this, and what lesson can we learn?

12. **Bonus**: Summarize four main lessons you learned from Joseph.

Workbook on Genesis

Printed books, booklets, and tracts available at
www.lighttomypath.net/sales
Free Bible study articles online at
www.gospelway.com
Free Bible courses online at
www.biblestudylessons.com
Free class books at
www.biblestudylessons.com/classbooks
Free commentaries on Bible books at
www.gospelway.com/commentary
Contact the author at
www.gospelway.com/comments
Free e-mail Bible study newsletter - www.gospelway.com/update_subscribe.htm

Made in the USA
Columbia, SC
06 November 2024